G. F. WATTS

THE HABIT DOES NOT MAKE THE MONK.

G. F. WATTS
BY G. K. CHESTERTON

38735

CHICAGO   NEW YORK
RAND, McNALLY & COMPANY

ND 497
W3

PRINTED IN GREAT BRITAIN AT
THE BALLANTYNE PRESS
LONDON

LIST OF PHOTOGRAVURES

Facing p.

THE HABIT DOES NOT MAKE THE MONK *Frontispiece*

G. F. WATTS, R.A. 8

THE RIDER ON THE WHITE HORSE 10

LESLIE STEPHEN 14

WALTER CRANE 16

THE SLUMBER OF THE AGES 18

CARDINAL MANNING 20

CHAOS 22

" FOR HE HAD GREAT POSSESSIONS " 26

AN IDLE CHILD OF FANCY 28

THE MINOTAUR 32

THE COURT OF DEATH 34

MATTHEW ARNOLD 36

JOHN STUART MILL 36

ROBERT BROWNING 38

LORD TENNYSON 38

THE DWELLER IN THE INNERMOST 40

GEORGE MEREDITH 42

ORPHEUS AND EURYDICE 44

HOPE 46

JONAH 48

LIST OF PHOTOGRAVURES

	Facing p.
MAMMON	52
DEATH CROWNING INNOCENCE	54
A STORY FROM BOCCACCIO	56
LORD LYTTON	58
DAWN	60
EVE REPENTANT	62
LOVE AND DEATH	64
WILLIAM MORRIS	66
DANTE GABRIEL ROSSETTI	68
THOMAS CARLYLE	70
GOOD LUCK TO YOUR FISHING	74

The Photogravures are from photographs by Fredk. Hollyer. Permanent photographs of works of Watts, Rossetti, Burne-Jones, Holbein, and of pictures in the Dublin and Hague Galleries can be obtained of Fredk. Hollyer, 9 Pembroke Square, Kensington.

G. F. WATTS, R.A.
Photograph from Life by Frederick Hollyer.

GEORGE FREDERICK WATTS was born on 23rd February 1817. His whole rise and career synchronizes roughly with the rise and career of the nineteenth century. As a rule, no doubt, such chronological parallels are peculiarly fanciful and unmeaning. Nothing can be imagined more idle, in a general way, than talking about a century as if it were some kind of animal with a head and tail, instead of an arbitrary length cut from an unending scroll. Nor is it less erroneous to assume that even if a period be definitely vital or disturbing, art must be a mirror of it ; the greatest political storm flutters only a fringe of humanity ; poets, like bricklayers, work on through a century of wars, and Bewick's birds, to take an instance, have the air of persons unaffected by the French Revolution. But in the case of Watts there are two circumstances which render the dates relevant. The first is that the nineteenth century was self-conscious, believed itself to be an idea and an atmosphere, and changed its name from a chronological almost to a philosophical term. I do not know whether all centuries do this or whether an advanced and progressive organ called " The Eleventh Century " was ever in contemplation in the dawn of the Middle Ages. But with us it is clear that a certain spirit was rightly or wrongly associated with the late century and that it called up images and thoughts like any historic or ritual date, like the Fourth of July or the First of April. What these images and thoughts were we shall be obliged in a few minutes and in the interests of the subject to inquire. But this is the first circumstance which renders the period important ; and the second is that it has always been so regarded by Watts himself. He, more than any other modern man, more than politicians who thundered on platforms or financiers who captured continents, has sought in the midst of his quiet and hidden life to mirror his age. He was born in the white and austere dawn of that great reforming century, and he has lingered after its grey and doubtful close. He is above all things a typical figure, a survival of the nineteenth century.

It will appear to many a somewhat grotesque matter to talk about a period in which most of us were born and which has only been dead a year or two, as if it were a primal Babylonian empire of which only a few columns are left crumbling in the desert. And yet such is, in spirit, the fact. There is no more remarkable psychological element in history than the way in which a period can suddenly become unintelligible. To the early Victorian period we have in a moment lost the key : the Crystal Palace is the temple of a forgotten creed. The thing always happens sharply : a whisper runs through the salons, Mr. Max Beerbohm waves a wand and a whole generation of great men and great achievement suddenly looks mildewed and unmeaning. We see precisely the same thing in that other great reaction towards art and the vanities, the Restoration of Charles II. In that hour both the great schools of faith and valour which had seemed either angels or devils to all men : the dreams of Strafford and the great High Churchmen on the one hand ; the Moslem frenzy of the English Commons, the worship of the English law upon the

THE RIDER ON THE WHITE HORSE

other ; both seemed distant and ridiculous. The new
Cavalier despised the old Cavalier even more than he
despised the Roundhead. The last stand of English
chivalry dwindled sharply to the solitary figure of the
absurd old country gentleman drinking wine out of an
absurd old flagon. The great roar of Roundhead
psalms which cried out that the God of Battles was
loose in English meadows shrank to a single snuffle.
The new and polite age saw the old and serious one
exactly as we see the early Victorian era : they saw it,
that is to say, not as splendid, not as disastrous, not as
fruitful, not as infamous, not as good or bad, but
simply as ugly. Just as we can see nothing about
Lord Shaftesbury but his hat, they could see nothing
about Cromwell but his nose. There is no doubt
of the shock and sharpness of the silent transition.
The only difference is that accordingly as we think
of man and his nature, according to our deepest
intuitions about things, we shall see in the Restoration
and the *fin de siècle* philosophy a man waking from a
turbid and pompous dream, or a man hurled from
heaven and the wars of the angels.

G. F. Watts is so deeply committed to, and so
unalterably steeped in, this early Victorian seriousness
and air of dealing with great matters, that unless we
sharply apprehend that spirit, and its difference from
our own, we shall misunderstand his work from the
outset. Splendid as is the art of Watts technically
or obviously considered, we shall yet find much in
it to perplex and betray us, unless we understand his
original theory and intention, a theory and intention
dyed deeply with the colours of a great period which
is gone. The great technical inequalities of his work,
its bursts of stupendous simplicity in colour and
design, its daring failures, its strange symbolical
portraits, all will mislead or bewilder if we have not

11

the thread of intention. In order to hold that,
we must hold something which runs through
and supports, as a string supports jewels, all the
wars and treaties and reforms of the nineteenth
century.

There are at least three essential and preliminary
points on which Watts is so completely at one with
the nineteenth century and so completely out of
accord with the twentieth, that it may be advisable
to state them briefly before we proceed to the narrower
but not more cogent facts of his life and growth.
The first of these is a nineteenth-century atmosphere
which is so difficult to describe, that we can only
convey it by a sort of paradox. It is difficult to
know whether it should be called doubt or faith.
For if, on the one hand, real faith would have been
more confident, real doubt, on the other hand, would
have been more indifferent. The attitude of that
age of which the middle and best parts of Watts'
work is most typical, was an attitude of devouring
and concentrated interest in things which were, by
their own system, impossible or unknowable. Men
were, in the main, agnostics : they said, " We do
not know " ; but not one of them ever ventured to
say, " We do not care." In most eras of revolt
and question, the sceptics reap something from their
scepticism : if a man were a believer in the eighteenth
century, there was Heaven ; if he were an unbeliever,
there was the Hell-Fire Club. But these men re-
strained themselves more than hermits for a hope
that was more than half hopeless, and sacrificed hope
itself for a liberty which they would not enjoy ; they
were rebels without deliverance and saints without
reward. There may have been and there was something arid and over-pompous about them : a newer
and gayer philosophy may be passing before us and

12

changing many things for the better; but we shall
not easily see any nobler race of men, and of them
all most assuredly there was none nobler than Watts.
If anyone wishes to see that spirit, he will see it in
pictures painted by Watts in a form beyond expression
sad and splendid. *Hope* that is dim and delicate
and yet immortal, the indestructible minimum of
the spirit; *Love and Death* that is awful and yet
the reverse of horrible; *The Court of Death* that is
like a page of Epictetus and might have been dreamt
by a dead Stoic : these are the visions of that spirit
and the incarnations of that time. Its faith was
doubtful, but its doubt was faithful. And its supreme
and acute difference from most periods of scepticism,
from the later Renaissance, from the Restoration
and from the hedonism of our own time was this,
that when the creeds crumbled and the gods seemed
to break up and vanish, it did not fall back, as we
do, on things yet more solid and definite, upon
art and wine and high finance and industrial
efficiency and vices. It fell in love with abstrac-
tions and became enamoured of great and desolate
words.

The second point of *rapport* between Watts and his
time was a more personal matter, a matter more
concerned with the man, or, at least, the type; but
it throws so much light upon almost every step of
his career that it may with advantage be suggested
here. Those who know the man himself, the
quaint and courtly old man down at Limnerslease,
know that if he has one trait more arresting
than another, it is his almost absurd humility. He
even disparages his own talent that he may insist
rather upon his aims. His speech and gesture are
simple, his manner polite to the point of being depre-
cating, his soul to all appearance of an almost con-

founding clarity and innocence. But although these appearances accurately represent the truth about him, though he is in reality modest and even fantastically modest, there is another element in him, an element which was in almost all the great men of his time, and it is something which many in these days would call a kind of splendid and inspired impudence. It is that wonderful if simple power of preaching, of claiming to be heard, of believing in an internal message and destiny : it is the audacious faculty of mounting a pulpit. Those would be very greatly mistaken who, misled by the child-like and humble manner of this monk of art, expected to find in him any sort of doubt, or any sort of fear, or any sort of modesty about the aims he follows or the cause he loves. He has the one great certainty which marks off all the great Victorians from those who have come after them : he may not be certain that he is successful, or certain that he is great, or certain that he is good, or certain that he is capable : but he is certain that he is right. It is of course the very element of confidence which has in our day become least common and least possible. We know we are brilliant and distinguished, but we do not know we are right. We swagger in fantastic artistic costumes ; we praise ourselves ; we fling epigrams right and left ; we have the courage to play the egoist and the courage to play the fool, but we have not the courage to preach. If we are to deliver a philosophy it must be in the manner of the late Mr. Whistler and the *ridentem dicere verum*. If our heart is to be aimed at it must be with the rapier of Stevenson which runs us through without either pain or puncture. It is only just to say, that good elements as well as bad ones have joined in making this old Victorian preaching difficult or alien to us.

14

LESLIE STEPHEN.

GEORGE FREDERICK WATTS

Humility as well as fear, camaraderie as well as cynicism, a sense of complexity and a kind of gay and worldly charity have led us to avoid the pose of the preacher, to be moral by ironies, to whisper a word and glide away. But, whatever may be the accidental advantage of this recoil from the didactic, it certainly does mean some loss of courage and of the old and athletic simplicity. Nay, in some sense it is really a loss of a fine pride and self-regard. Mr. Whistler coquetted and bargained about the position and sale of his pictures : he praised them ; he set huge prices on them ; but still under all disguise, he treated them as trifles. Watts, when scarcely more than a boy and comparatively unknown, started his great custom of offering his pictures as gifts worthy of a great nation. Thus we came to the conclusion, a conclusion which may seem to some to contain a faint element of paradox, that Mr. Whistler suffered from an excessive and exaggerated modesty. And this unnatural modesty of Mr. Whistler can scarcely be more typically symbolized than in his horror of preaching. The new school of art and thought does indeed wear an air of audacity, and breaks out everywhere into blasphemies, as if it required any courage to say a blasphemy. There is only one thing that it requires real courage to say, and that is a truism.

Lastly, it would be quite impossible to complete this prefatory suggestion of the atmosphere in which the mind of Watts grew and prevailed, without saying something about that weary and weather-beaten question of the relation of art to ethics on which so much has been said in connexion with him and his contemporaries. About the real aim and the real value of Watts' allegorical pictures I shall speak later, but for the moment it is only desirable to point out what the early and middle Victorian view of

15

the matter really was. According to the later
æsthetic creed which Mr. Whistler and others did
so much to preach, the state of the arts under the
reign of that Victorian view was a chaos of everyone minding everyone else's business. It was a
world in which painters were trying to be novelists,
and novelists trying to be historians, and musicians
doing the work of schoolmasters, and sculptors doing
the work of curates. That is a view which has some
truth in it, both as a description of the actual state of
things and as involving an interesting and suggestive
philosophy of the arts. But a good deal of harm
may be done by ceaselessly repeating to ourselves
even a true and fascinating fashionable theory, and a
great deal of good by endeavouring to realize the real
truth about an older one. The thing from which
England suffers just now more than from any other
evil is not the assertion of falsehoods, but the endless
and irrepressible repetition of half-truths. There is
another side to every historic situation, and that
often a startling one; and the other side of the
Victorian view of art, now so out of mode, is too
little considered. The salient and essential characteristic of Watts and men of his school was that they
regarded life as a whole. They had in their heads, as
it were, a synthetic philosophy which put everything
into a certain relation with God and the wheel of
things. Thus, psychologically speaking, they were
incapable not merely of holding such an opinion,
but actually of thinking such a thought as that of art
for art's sake; it was to them like talking about
voting for voting's sake, or amputating for amputating's
sake. To them as to the ancient Jews the Spirit of
the unity of existence declared in thunder that
they should not make any graven image, or have any
gods but Him. Doubtless, they did not give art a

WALTER CRANE.

relation of unimpeachable correctness : in their scheme of things it may be true, or rather it is true, that the æsthetic was confused with the utilitarian, that good gardens were turned so to speak into bad cornfields, and a valuable temple into a useless post-office. But in so far as they had this fundamental idea that art must be linked to life, and to the strength and honour of nations, they were a hundred times more broad-minded and more right than the new ultra-technical school. The idea of following art through everything for itself alone, through extravagance, through cruelty, through morbidity, is just exactly as superstitious as the idea of following theology for itself alone through extravagance and cruelty and morbidity. To deny that Baudelaire is loathsome, or Nietzsche inhuman, because we stand in awe of beauty, is just the same thing as denying that the Court of Pope Julius was loathsome, or the rack inhuman, because we stand in awe of religion. It is not necessary and it is not honest. The young critics of the Green Carnation, with their nuances and technical mysteries, would doubtless be surprised to learn that as a class they resemble ecstatic nuns, but their principle is, in reality, the same. There is a great deal to be said for them, and a great deal, for that matter, to be said for nuns. But there is nothing to be surprised at, nothing to call for any charge of inconsistency or lack of enlightenment, about the conduct of Watts and the great men of his age, in being unable to separate art from ethics. They were nationalists and universalists : they thought that the ecstatic isolation of the religious sense had done incalculable harm to religion. It is not remarkable or unreasonable that they should think that the ecstatic isolation of the artistic sense would do incalculable harm to art.

This, then, was the atmosphere of Watts and

Victorian idealism : an atmosphere so completely vanished from the world of art in which we now live that the above somewhat long introduction is really needed to make it vivid or human to us. These three elements may legitimately, as I have said, be predicated of it as its main characteristics : first, the sceptical idealism, the belief that abstract verities remained the chief affairs of men when theology left them ; second, the didactic simplicity, the claim to teach other men and to assume one's own value and rectitude ; third, the cosmic utilitarianism, the consideration of any such thing as art or philosophy perpetually with reference to a general good. They may be right or wrong, they may be returning or gone for ever ; theories and fashions may change the face of humanity again and yet again ; but at least in that one old man at Limnerslease, burned, and burned until death, these convictions, like three lamps in an old pagan temple of stoicism.

Of the ancestry of Watts so little is known that it resolves itself into one hypothesis : a hypothesis which brings with it a suggestion, a suggestion employed by almost all his existing biographers, but a suggestion which cannot, I think, pass unchallenged, although the matter may appear somewhat theoretic and remote. Watts was born in London, but his family had in the previous generation come from Hereford. The vast amount of Welsh blood which is by the nature of the case to be found in Herefordshire has led to the statement that Watts is racially a Celt, which is very probably true. But it is also said, in almost every notice of his life and work, that the Celtic spirit can be detected in his painting, that the Celtic principle of mysticism is a characteristic of his artistic conceptions. It is in no idly antagonistic spirit that I venture to doubt this most profoundly.

18

THE SLUMBER OF THE AGES

GEORGE FREDERICK WATTS

Watts may or may not be racially a Celt, but there is nothing Celtic about his mysticism. The essential Celtic spirit in letters and art may, I think, be defined as a sense of the unbearable beauty of things. The essential spirit of Watts may, I think, be much better expressed as a sense of the joyful austerity of things. The dominant passion of the artistic Celt, of Mr. W. B. Yeats or Sir Edward Burne-Jones, is in the word "escape": escape into a land where oranges grow on plum-trees and m can sow what they like and reap what they enjoy. To Watts the very word "escape" would be horrible, like an obscene word: his ideal is altogether duty and the great wheel. To the Celt frivolity is most truly the most serious of things, since in the tangle of roses is always the old serpent who is wiser than the world. To Watts seriousness is most truly the most "joyful of things," since in it we come nearest to that ultimate equilibrium and reconciliation of things whereby alone they live and endure life and each other. It is difficult to imagine that amid all the varieties of noble temper and elemental desire there could possibly be two exhibiting a more total divergence than that between a kindly severity and an almost cruel love of sweetness; than that between a laborious and open-air charity and a kind of Bacchic asceticism; between a joy in peace and a joy in disorder; between a reduction of existence to its simplest formula and an extension of t to its most frantic corollary; between a lover of justice who accepts the real world more submissively than a slave and a lover of pleasure who despises the real world more bitterly than a hermit; between a king in battle-harness and a vagabond in elf-land; between Watts and Sir Edward Burne-Jones.

It is remarkable that even the technical style of Watts gives a contradiction to this Celtic theory.

19

Watts is strong precisely where the Celt is weak, and weak precisely where the Celt is strong. The only thing that the Celt has lacked in art is that hard mass, that naked outline, that ἀρχιτεκτονική, which makes Watts a sort of sculptor of draughtsmanship. It is as well for us that the Celt has not had this : if he had, he would rule the world with a rod of iron for he has everything else. There are no hard blac lines in Burke's orations, or Tom Moore's songs, or th plays of Mr. W. B. Yeats. Burke is the greatest o political philosophers, because in him only are ther distances and perspectives, as there are on the rea earth, with its mists of morning and evening, and it blue horizons and broken skies. Moore's songs have neither a pure style nor deep realization, nor origi nality of form, nor thought nor wit nor vigour, bu they h e something else which is none of these things which is nameless and the one thing needful. In Mr Yeats' plays there is only one character : the herd who rules and kills all the others, and his name i Atmosphere. Atmosphere and the gleaming distance are the soul of Celtic greatness as they were of Burne Jones, who was, as I have said, weak precisely where Watts is strong, in the statuesque quality in drawing in the love of heavy hands like those of *Mammon* of a strong back like that of *Eve Repentant*, in a single fearless and austere outline like that of the angel in *The Court of Death*, in the frame-filling violence o *Jonah*, in the half-witted brutality of *The Minotaur* He is deficient, that is to say, in what can only be called the god-like materialism of art. Watts, on the othe hand, is peculiarly strong in it. Idealist as he is there is nothing frail or phantasmal about the things or the figures he loves. Though not himself a robust man, he loves robustness ; he loves a great bulk of shoulder, an abrupt bend of neck, a gigantic stride,

CARDINAL MANNING.

a large and swinging limb, a breast bound as with bands of brass. Of course the deficiency in such a case is very far from being altogether on one side. There are abysses in Burne-Jones which Watts could not understand, the Celtic madness, older than any sanity, the hunger that will remain after the longest feast, the sorrow that is built up of stratified delights. From the point of view of the true Celt, Watts, the Watts who painted the great stoical pictures *Love and Death*, *Time*, *Death and Judgment*, *The Court of Death*, *Mammon*, and *Cain*, this pictorial Watts would probably be, must almost certainly be, simply a sad, sane, strong, stupid Englishman. He may or may not be Welsh by extraction or by part of his extraction, but in spirit he is an Englishman, with all the faults and all the disadvantages of an Englishman. He is a great Englishman like Milton or Gladstone, of the type, that is to say, that were too much alive for anything but gravity, and who enjoyed themselves far too much to trouble to enjoy a joke. Matthew Arnold has come near to defining that kind of idealism, so utterly different from the Celtic kind, which is to be found in Milton and again in Watts. He has called it, in one of his finest and most accurate phrases, "the imaginative reason."

This racial legend about the Watts family does not seem to rest upon any certain foundations, and as I have said, the deduction drawn from it is quite loose and misleading. The whole is only another example of that unfortunate, if not infamous, modern habit of talking about such things as heredity with a vague notion that science has closed the question when she has only just opened it. Nobody knows, as a matter of fact, whether a Celtic mysticism can be inherited any more than a theory on the Education Bill. But the eagerness of the popular mind to snatch

at a certainty is too impatient for the tardy processes
of real hypothesis and research. Long before heredity
has become a science, it has become a superstition.
And this curious though incidental case of the
origin of the Watts genius is just one of those cases
which make us wonder what has been the real result
of the great rise of science. So far the result would
painfully appear to be that whereas men in the earlier
times said unscientific things with the vagueness of
gossip and legend, they now say unscientific things
with the plainness and the certainty of science.

The actual artistic education of Watts, though
thorough indeed in its way, had a somewhat peculiar
character, the air of something detached and private,
and to the external eye something even at random.
He works hard, but in an elusive and personal manner.
He does not remember the time when he did not
draw : he was an artist in his babyhood as he is an
artist still in his old age. Like Ruskin and many other
of the great and serious men of the century, he would
seem to have been brought up chiefly on what may be
called the large legendary literature, on such as Homer
and Scott. Among his earliest recorded works was
a set of coloured illustrations to the Waverley Novels
and a sketch of the struggle for the body of Patroclus.
He went to the Academy schools, but only stayed
there about a month ; never caring for or absorbing
the teaching, such as it was, of the place. He wan-
dered perpetually in the Greek galleries of the British
Museum, staring at the Elgin marbles, from which
he always declared he learnt all the art he knew.
" There," he said, stretching out his hand towards
the Ilyssus in his studio, " there is my master."
We hear of a friendship between him and the sculptor
William Behnes, of Watts lounging about that artist's
studio, playing with clay, modelling busts, and staring

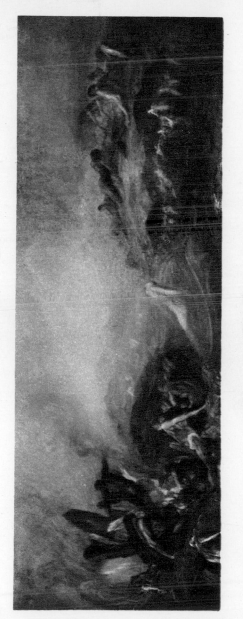

CHAOS.

at the work of sculpture. His eyes seemed to have been at this time the largest and hungriest part of him. Even when the great chance and first triumph of his life arrived a year or two later, even when he gained the great scholarship which sent him abroad to work amid the marbles of Italy, when a famous ambassador was his patron and a brilliant circle his encouragement, we do not find anything of the conventional student about him. He never painted in the galleries; he only dreamed in them. This must not, of course, be held to mean that he did not work; though one or two people who have written memoirs of Watts have used a phraseology, probably without noticing it, which might be held to imply this. Not only is the thing ludicrously incongruous with his exact character and morals; but anyone who knows anything whatever about the nature of pictorial art will know quite well that a man could not paint like that without having worked; just as he would know that a man could not be the Living Serpent without any previous practice with his joints. To say that he could really learn to paint and draw with the technical merit of Watts, or with any technical merit at all, by simply looking at other people's pictures and statues will seem to anyone, with a small technical sense, like saying that a man learnt to be a sublime violinist by staring at fiddles in a shop window. It is as near a physical impossibility as can exist in these matters. Work Watts must have done and did do; it is the only conclusion possible which is consistent either with the nature of Watts or the nature of painting; and it is fully supported by the facts. But what the facts do reveal is that he worked in this curiously individual, this curiously invisible way. He had his own notion of when to dream and when to draw; as he shrank

from no toil, so he shrank from no idleness. He was
something which is one of the most powerful and
successful things in the world, something which is far
more powerful and successful than a legion of students
and prizemen : he was a serious and industrious
truant.

It is worth while to note this in his boyhood,
partly, of course, because from one end of his life to
the other there is this queer note of loneliness and
liberty. But it is also more immediately and prac-
tically important because it throws some light on the
development and character of his art, and even
especially of his technique. The great singularity
of Watts, considered as a mere artist, is that he stands
alone. He is not connected with any of the groups
of the nineteenth century : he has neither followed a
school nor founded one. He is not mediæval; but
no one could exactly call him classical : we have only
to compare him to Leighton to feel the difference at
once. His artistic style is rather a thing more primitive than paganism ; a thing to which paganism
and mediævalism are alike upstart sects ; a style of
painting there might have been upon the tower of
Babel. He is mystical; but he is not mediæval :
we have only to compare him to Rossetti to feel the
difference. When he emerged into the artistic world,
that world was occupied by the pompous and historical school, that school which was so exquisitely
caricatured by Thackeray in Gandish and his
" Boadishia " ; but Watts was not pompous or
historical : he painted one historical picture, which
brought him a youthful success, and he has scarcely
painted another. He lived on through the great
Pre-Raphaelite time, that very noble and very much
undervalued time, when men found again what had
been hidden since the thirteenth century under loads

of idle civilization, the truth that simplicity and a monastic laboriousness is the happiest of all things ; the great truth that purity is the only atmosphere for passion ; the great truth that silver is more beautiful than gold. But though there is any quantity of this sentiment in Watts himself, Watts never has been a Pre-Raphaelite. He has seen other fashions come and go ; he has seen the Pre-Raphaelites overwhelmed by a heavy restoration of the conventional, headed by Millais with his Scotch moors and his English countesses ; but he has not heeded it. He has seen these again overturned by the wild lancers of Whistler ; he has seen the mists of Impressionism settle down over the world, making it weird and delicate and non-committal : but he thinks no more of the wet mist of the Impressionist than he thought of the dry glare of the Pre-Raphaelite.

He, the most mild of men, has yet never been anything but Watts. He has followed the gleam, like some odd modern Merlin. He has escaped all the great atmospheres, the divine if deluding intoxications, which have whirled one man one way and one another ; which flew to the head of a perfect stylist like Ruskin and made him an insane scientist ; which flew to the head of a great artist like Whistler and made him a pessimistic dandy. He has passed them with a curious immunity, an immunity which, if it were not so nakedly innocent, might almost be called egotism ; but which is in fact rather the single eye. He said once that he had not even consented to illustrate a book ; his limitation was that he could express no ideas but his own. He admired Tennyson ; he thought him the greatest of poets ; he thought him a far greater man than himself ; he read him, he adored him, but he could not illustrate him. This is the curious secret strength which kept him inde-

25

pendent in his youth and kept him independent through the great roaring triumph of the Pre-Raphaelite and the great roaring triumph of the Impressionist. He stands in the world of art as he stood in the studio of Behnes and in the Uffizi Gallery. He stands gazing, but not copying.

Of Watts as he was at this time there remains a very interesting portrait painted by himself. It represents him at the age of nineteen, a dark, slim, and very boyish-looking creature. Something in changed conditions may no doubt account for the flowing and voluminous dark hair : we see such a mane in many of the portraits of the most distinguished men of that time ; but if a man appeared now and walked down Fleet Street with so neglected a *hure*, he would be mistaken for an advertisement of a hair-dresser, or by the more malicious for a minor poet. But there is about this picture not a trace of affectation or the artistic immunity in these matters : the boy's dress is rough and ordinary, his expression is simple and unconscious. From a modern standpoint we should say without hesitation that if his hair is long it is because he has forgotten to have it cut. And there is something about this contrast between the unconsciously leonine hair and the innocent and almost bashful face, there is something like a parable of Watts. His air is artistic, if you will. His famous skull cap, which makes him look like a Venetian senator, is as pictorial and effective as the boyish mane in the picture. But he belongs to that older race of Bohemians, of which even Thackeray only saw the sunset, the great old race of art and literature who were ragged because they were really poor, frank because they were really free, and untidy because they were really forgetful. It will not do to confuse Watts with these men ; there is

26

"FOR HE HAD GREAT POSSESSIONS."

much about him that is precise and courtly, and
which, as I shall have occasion to remark, belongs
really to a yet older period. But it is more right to
reckon Watts along with them in their genuine
raggedness than to suppose that the unquestionable
picturesqueness with which he fronts the world has
any relation with that new Bohemianism which is
untidy because it is conventional, frank because it
follows a fashion, careless because it watches for all
its effects, and ragged and coarse in its tastes because
it has too much money.

The first definite encouragement, or at least the
first encouragement now ascertainable, probably came
to the painter from that interesting Greek amateur,
Mr. Constantine Ionides. It was under his encouragement that Watts began all his earlier work of the more
ambitious kind, and it was the portrait of Mrs. Constantine Ionides which ranks among the earliest of his
definite successes. He achieved immediate profes-
sional success, however, at an astonishingly early age,
judged by modern standards. When he was barely
twenty he had three pictures in the Royal Academy :
the first two were portraits, and the third a picture
called *The Wounded Heron*. There is always a very
considerable temptation to fantasticality in dealing
with these artistic origins : no doubt it does not
always follow that a man is destined to be a military
conqueror because he beats other little boys at school,
nor endued with a passionate and clamorous nature
because he begins this mortal life with a yell. But
Watts has, to a rather unusual degree, a sincere and
consistent and homogeneous nature ; and this first
exhibit of his has really a certain amount of symbolism
about it. Portraiture, with which he thus began, he
was destined to raise to a level never before attained
in English art, so far as significance and humanity

are concerned ; and there is really something a little fascinating about the fact that along with these pictures went one picture which had, for all practical purposes, an avowedly humanitarian object. The picture of *The Wounded Heron* scarcely ever attracts attention, I imagine, in these days, but it may, of course, have been recalled for a moment to the popular mind by that curious incident which occurred in connexion with it and which has often been told. Long after the painter who produced that picture in his struggling boyhood had lost sight of it and in all probability forgotten all about its existence, a chance traveller with a taste in the arts happened to find it in the dusty curiosity-shop of a north-country town. He bought it and gave it back to the now celebrated painter, who hung it among the exhibits at Little Holland House. It is, as I have said, a thing painted clearly with a humanitarian object : it depicts the suffering of a stricken creature ; it depicts the helplessness of life under the cruelty of the inanimate violence ; it depicts the pathos of dying and the greater pathos of living. Since then, no doubt, Watts has improved his machinery of presentation and found larger and more awful things to tell his tale with than a bleeding bird. The wings of the heron have widened till they embrace the world with the terrible wings of Time or Death : he has summoned the stars to help him and sent the angels as his ambassadors. He has changed the plan of operations until it includes Heaven and Tartarus. He has never changed the theme.

The relations of Watts to Constantine Ionides either arose or became important about this time. The painter's fortunes rose quickly and steadily, so far as the Academy was concerned. He continued to exhibit with a fair amount of regularity, chiefly in the form of subjects from the great romantic or

AN IDLE CHILD OF FANCY.

historic traditions which were then the whole pabulum of the young idealistic artist. In the Academy of 1840 came a picture on the old romantic subject of Ferdinand and Isabella; in the following year but one, a picture on the old romantic subject of Cymbeline. The portrait of Mrs. Constantine Ionides appeared in 1842.

But Watts' mode of thought from the very beginning had very little kinship with the Academy and very little kinship with this kind of private and conventional art. An event was shortly to occur, the first success of his life, but an event far less important when considered as the first success of his life than it is when considered as an essential characteristic of his mind. The circumstances are so extremely characteristic of something in the whole spirit of the man's art that it may be permissible to dwell at length on the significance of the fact rather than on the fact itself.

The great English Parliament, the Senate that broke the English kings, had just moved its centre of existence. The new Houses of Parliament had opened with what seemed to the men of that time an opening world. A competition was started for the decoration of the halls, and Watts suddenly sprang into importance: he won the great prize. The cartoon of *Caractacus led in triumph through the streets of Rome* was accepted from this almost nameless man by the great central power of English history. And until we have understood that fact we have not understood Watts: it was (one may be permitted to fancy) the supreme hour of his life. For Watts' nature is essentially public—that is to say, it is modest and noble, and has nothing to hide. His art is an outdoor art, like that of the healthy ages of the world, like the statuesque art of Greece, like the ecclesiastical and external Gothic art of Christianity: an art that can look the sun in the face. He ought to be employed to paint factory chimneys and railway stations. I know that this will sound like an insolence : my only answer is that he, in accordance with this great conception of his, actually offered to paint a railway station. With a splendid and truly religious imagination, he asked permission to decorate Euston. The railway managers (not perceiving, in their dull classical routine, the wild poetry of their own station) declined. But until we have understood this immense notion of publicity in the soul of Watts, we have understood nothing. The fundamental modern fallacy is that the public life must be an artificial life. It is like saying that the public street must be an artificial air. Men like Watts, men like all the great heroes, only breathe in public. What is the use of abusing a man for publicity when he utters in public the true and the enduring things ? What is the use, above all, of prying into his secrecy when he has cried his best from the house-tops ?

This is the real argument which makes a detailed biography of Watts unnecessary for all practical purposes. It is in vain to climb walls and hide in cupboards in order to show whether Watts eats mustard or pepper with his curry or whether Watts takes sugar or salt with his porridge. These things may or may not become public : it matters little. The innermost that the biographer could at last discover, after all possible creepings and capers, would be what Watts in his inmost soul believes, and that Watts has splashed on twenty feet of canvas and given to the nation for nothing. Like one of the great orators of the eighteenth century, his public virtues, his public ecstasies are far more really significant than his private weaknesses. The rest of his life is so simple that it is scarcely worth telling. He went

with the great scholarship he gained with his *Caractacus*
to Italy. There he found a new patron—the famous
Lord Holland, with the whole of whose great literary
circle he rapidly became acquainted. He painted
many of his most famous portraits in connexion with
this circle, both in Italy and afterwards in Paris. But
this great vision of the public idea had entered his
blood. He offered his cartoons to Euston Station;
he painted St. George and the Dragon for the House
of Lords; he presented a fresco to the great hall
at Lincoln's Inn. Of his life there is scarcely more
to say, except the splendid fact that he three times
refused a title. Of his character there is a great deal
more to say.

There is unquestionably about the personal attitude
of Watts something that in the vague phraseology
of modern times would be called Puritan. Puritan,
however, is very far from being really the right word.
The right word is a word which has been singularly
little used in English nomenclature because historical
circumstances have separated us from the origin
from which it sprang. The right word for the spirit
of Watts is *Stoicism*. Watts is at one with the Puritans
in the actual objects of his attack. One of his deepest
and most enduring troubles, a matter of which he
speaks and writes frequently, is the prevalence of
gambling. With the realism of an enthusiast, he
has detected the essential fact that the problem of
gambling is even more of a problem in the case of the
poorer classes than in the case of the richer. It is,
as he asserts, a far worse danger than drink. There
are many other instances of his political identity
with Puritanism. He told Mr. W. T. Stead that
he had defended and was prepared to defend the
staggering publications of the " Maiden Tribute ";
it was the only way, he said, to stem the evil. A

picturesque irradiation asserts indeed that it was under the glow of Hebraic anger against these Babylonian cruelties of Piccadilly and the Strand that he painted as a symbol of those cruelties that brutal and magnificent picture *The Minotaur*. The pictures themselves of course bear sufficient attestation to this general character : *Mammon* is what we call a Puritan picture, and *Jonah*, and *Fata Morgana*, and *For he had Great Possessions*. It is not difficult to see that Watts has the Puritan vigilance, the Puritan realism, and the Puritan severity in his attitude towards public affairs. Nevertheless, as I have said, he is to be described rather as a Stoic than a Puritan. The essential difference between Christian and Pagan asceticism lies in the fact that Paganism in renouncing pleasure gives up something which it does not think desirable ; whereas Christianity in giving up pleasure gives up something which it thinks very desirable indeed. Thus there is a frenzy in Christian asceticism ; its follies and renunciations are like those of first love. There is a passion, and as it were a regret, in the Puritanism of Bunyan ; there is none in the Puritanism of Watts. He is not Bunyan, he is Cato. The difference may be a difficult one to convey, but it is one that must not be ignored or great misunderstandings will follow. The one self-abnegation is more reasonable but less joyful. The Stoic casts away pleasure like the parings of his nails ; the Mystic cuts it off like his right hand that offends him. In Watts we have the noble self-abnegation of a noble type and school ; but everything, however noble, that has shape has limitation, and we must not look in Watts, with his national self-mastery, either for the nightmare of Stylites or the gaiety of Francis of Assisi.

It has already been remarked that the chief note

of the painter's character is a certain mixture of
personal delicacy and self-effacement with the most
immense and audacious aims. But it is so essential
a trait that it will bear a repetition and the introduction of a curious example of it. Watts in his
quaint and even shy manner of speech often let
fall in conversation words which hint at a certain
principle or practice of his, a principle and practice
which are, when properly apprehended, beyond
expression impressive and daring. The spectator
who studies his allegorical paintings one after another
will be vaguely impressed with something uniquely
absent, something which is usual and familiar in such
pictures conspicuous by its withdrawal; a blank or
difference which makes them things sundered altogether from the millions of allegorical pictures that
throng the great and small galleries of painting. At
length the nature of this missing thing may suddenly
strike him : in the whole range of Watts' symbolic
art there is scarcely a single example of the ordinary
and arbitrary current symbol, the ecclesiastical symbol,
the heraldic symbol, the national symbol. A primeval
vagueness and archaism hang over all the canvases
and cartoons, like frescoes from some prehistoric
temple. There is nothing there but the eternal
things, clay and fire and the sea, and motherhood
and the dead. We cannot imagine the rose or the
lion of England ; the keys or the tiara of Rome ; the
red cap of Liberty or the crescent of Islam in a picture
by Watts ; we cannot imagine the Cross itself. And in
light and broken phrases, carelessly and humbly expressed, as I have said, the painter has admitted that
his great omission was observed on principle. Its
object is that the pictures may be intelligible if they
survive the whole modern order. Its object is, that
is to say, that if some savage in a dim futurity dug

up one of these dark designs on a lonely mountain, though he worshipped strange gods and served laws yet unwritten, it might strike the same message to his soul that it strikes upon clerks and navvies from the walls of the Tate Gallery. It is impossible not to feel a movement of admiration for the magnitude of the thought. Here is a man whose self-depreciation is internal and vital ; whose life is cloistered, whose character is childlike, and he has yet within such an unconscious and colossal sense of greatness that he paints on the assumption that his work may outlast the cross of the Eternal City. As a boy he scarcely expected worldly success : as an old man he still said that his worldly success had astonished him. But in his nameless youth and in his silent old age he paint like one upon a tower looking down the appalling per spective of the centuries towards fantastic temple and inconceivable republics.

This union of small self-esteem with a vast ambitio is a paradox in the very soul of the painter ; and whe we look at the symbolic pictures in the light of th theory of his, it is interesting and typical to observ how consistently he pursues any intellectual rul that he laid down for himself. An æsthetic ethical notion of this kind is not to him, as to mos men with the artistic temperament, a thing to ta about sumptuously, to develop in lectures, and t observe when it happens to be suitable. It is a thin like his early rising or his personal conscience, a thin which is either a rule or nothing. And we find th insistence on universal symbols, this rejection of symbols that are local or temporary or topical, eve if the locality be a whole continent, the time a stretc of centuries, or the topic a vast civilization or undying church—we find this insistence looking o very clearly from the allegories of Watts. It wou

34

THE COURT OF DEATH.

have been easy and effective, as he himself often said, to make the meaning of a picture clear by the introduction of some popular and immediate image : and it must constantly be remembered that Watts does care very much for making the meaning of his pictures clear. His work indeed has, as I shall suggest shortly, a far more subtle and unnamable quality than the merely hard and didactic ; but it must not be for one moment pretended that Watts does not claim to teach : to do so would be to falsify the man's life. And it would be easy, as is quite obvious, to make the pictures clearer : to hang a crucifix over the *Happy Warrior*, to give *Mammon* some imperial crown or typical heraldic symbols, to give a theological machinery to *The Court of Death*. But this is put on one side like a temptation of the flesh, because it conflicts with this stupendous idea of painting for all peoples and all centuries. I am not saying that this extraordinary ambition is necessarily the right view of art, or the right view of life. I am only reiterating it as an absolute trait of men of the time and type and temper of Watts. It may plausibly be maintained, I am not sure that it cannot more truly be maintained, that man cannot achieve and need not achieve this frantic universality. A man, I fancy, is after all only an animal that has noble preferences. It is the very difference between the artistic mind and the mathematical that the former sees things as they are in a picture, some nearer and larger, some smaller and further away : while to the mathematical mind everything, every unit in a million, every fact in a cosmos, must be of equal value. That is why mathematicians go mad ; and poets scarcely ever do. A man may have as wide a view of life as he likes, the wider the better; a distant view, a bird's-eye view, if he will, but still a view and not a map.

35

The one thing he cannot attempt in his version of the universe is to draw things to scale. I have put myself for a moment outside this universalism and doubted its validity because a thing always appears more sharp and personal and picturesque if we do not wholly agree with it. And this universalism is an essential and dominant feature of such great men as Watts and of his time as a whole. Mr. Herbert Spencer is a respectable, almost a dapper, figure, his theory is agnostic and his tone polite and precise. And yet he threw himself into a task more insane and gigantic than that of Dante, an inventory or plan of the universe itself; the awful vision of existence as a single organism, like an amœba on the disc of a microscope. He claimed, by implication, to put in their right places the flaming certainty of the martyrs, the wild novelties of the modern world; to arrange the eternal rock of Peter and the unbroken trance of Buddhism. It is only in this age of specialists, of cryptic experiences in art and faith like the present, that we can see how huge was that enterprise; but the spirit of it is the spirit of Watts. The man of that aggressive nineteenth century had many wild thoughts, but there was one thought that never even for an instant strayed across his burning brain. He never once thought, " Why should I understand the cat, any more than the cat understands me ? " He never thought, " Why should I be just to the merits of a Chinaman, any more than a pig studies the mystic virtues of a camel ? " He affronted heaven and the angels, but there was one hard arrogant dogma that he never doubted even when he doubted Godhead : he never doubted that he himself was as central and as responsible as God.

This paradox, then, we call the first element in the artistic and personal claim of Watts, that he

MATTHEW ARNOLD.

JOHN STUART MILL.

realizes the great paradox of the Gospel. He is meek, but he claims to inherit the earth. But there is, of course, a great deal more to be said before this view of the matter can be considered complete. The universalism preached by Watts and the other great Victorians was of course subject to certain specialisations; it is not necessary to call them limitations. Like Matthew Arnold, the last and most sceptical of them, who expressed their basic idea in its most detached and philosophic form, they held that conduct was three-fourths of life. They were ingrainedly ethical; the mere idea of thinking anything more important than ethics would have struck them as profane. In this they were certainly right, but they were nevertheless partial or partisan; they did not really maintain the judicial attitude of the universalist. The mere thought of Watts painting a picture called *The Victory of Joy over Morality*, or *Nature rebuking Conscience*, is enough to show the definite limits of that cosmic equality. This is not, of course, to be taken as a fault in the attitude of Watts. He simply draws the line somewhere, as all men, including anarchists, draw it somewhere; he is dogmatic, as all sane men are dogmatic.

There is another phase of this innocent audacity. It may appear to be more fanciful, it is certainly more completely a matter of inference; but it throws light on yet another side of the character of Watts.

Watts' relation to friends and friendship has something about it very typical. He is not a man desirous or capable of a very large or rich or varied circle of acquaintance. There is nothing Bohemian about him. He belongs both chronologically and psychologically to that period which is earlier even than Thackeray and his Cave of Harmony : he belongs to the quiet, struggling, self-created men of the forties, with their tradition of self-abnegating individualism. Much as there is about him of the artist and the poet, there is something about him also of the industrious apprentice. That strenuous solitude in which Archbishop Temple as a boy struggled to carry a bag of ironmongery which crushed his back, in which Gladstone cut down trees and John Stuart Mill read half the books of the world in boyhood, that strenuous solitude entered to some degree into the very soul of Watts and made him independent of them. But the friends he made have as a general rule been very characteristic : they have marked the strange and haughty fastidiousness that goes along with his simplicity. His friends, his intimate friends, that is, have been marked by a certain indescribable and stately worthiness : more than one of them have been great men like himself. The greatest and most intimate of all his friends, probably, was Tennyson, and in this there is something singularly characteristic of Watts. About the actuality of the intellectual tie that bound him to Tennyson there can be little doubt. He painted three, if not four, portraits of him ; his name was often on his lips ; he invoked him always as the typical great poet, excusing his faults and expounding his virtues. He invoked his authority as that of the purest of poets, and invoked it very finely and well in a sharp controversial interview he had on the nature and ethics of the nude in art.

At the time I write, there is standing at the end of the garden at Limnerslease a vast shed, used for a kind of sculptor's studio, in which there stands a splendid but unfinished statue, on which the veteran of the arts is even now at work. It represents Tennyson, wrapped in his famous mantle, with his magnificent head bowed, gazing at something in the

38

ROBERT BROWNING.

LORD TENNYSON

hollow of his hand. The subject is *Flower in the Crannied Wall*. There is something very characteristic of Watts in the contrast between the colossal plan of the figure and the smallness of the central object.

But while the practical nature of the friendship between Watts and Tennyson is clear enough, there is something really significant, something really relevant to Watts' attitude in its ultimate and psychological character. It is surely most likely that Watts and Tennyson were drawn together because they both represented a certain relation towards their art which is not common in our time and was scarcely properly an attribute of any artists except these two. Watts could not have found the thing he most believed in Browning or Swinburne or Morris or any of the other poets. Tennyson could not have found the thing he most believed in Leighton or Millais or any of the other painters. They were brought together, it must be supposed, by the one thing that they had really in common, a profound belief in the solemnity, the ceremoniousness, the responsibility, and what most men would now, in all probability, call the pomposity of the great arts.

Watts has always a singular kind of semi-mystical tact in the matter of portrait painting. His portraits are commonly very faultless comments and have the same kind of superlative mental delicacy that we see in the picture of *Hope*. And the whole truth of this last matter is very well expressed in Watts' famous portrait of Tennyson, particularly if we look at it in conjunction with his portrait of Browning. The head of Browning is the head of a strong, splendid, joyful, and anxious man who could write magnificent poetry. The head of Tennyson is the head of a poet. Watts has painted Tennyson with his dark

dome-like head relieved against a symbolic green and
blue of the eternal sea and the eternal laurels. He
has behind him the bays of Dante and he is wrapped
in the cloak of the prophets. Browning is dressed
like an ordinary modern man, and we at once feel
that it should and must be so. To dress Browning
in the prophet's robe and the poet's wreath would
strike us all as suddenly ridiculous; it would be like
sending him to a fancy-dress ball. It would be like
attiring Matthew Arnold in the slashed tights of an
Elizabethan, or putting Mr. Lecky into a primitive
Celto-Irish kilt. But it does not strike us as absurd
in the case of Tennyson: it does not strike us as even
eccentric or outlandish or remote. We think of
Tennyson in that way; we think of him as a lordly
and conscious bard. Some part of this fact may,
of course, be due to his possession of a magnificent
physical presence; but not, I think, all. Lord
Kitchener (let us say) is a handsome man, but we
should laugh at him very much in silver armour.
It is much more due to the fact that Tennyson
really assumed and was granted this stately and epic
position. It is not true that Tennyson was more of
a poet than Browning, if we mean by that statement
that Browning could not compose forms as artistic
and well-managed, lyrics as light and poignant, and
rhythms as swelling and stirring as any in English
letters. But it is true that Tennyson was more of a
poet than Browning, if we mean by that statement
that Tennyson was a poet in person, in post and circumstance and conception of life; and that Browning
was not, in that sense, a poet at all. Browning first
inaugurated in modern art and letters the notion or
tradition, in many ways perhaps a more wholesome
one, that the fact that a man pursued the trade or
practice of poetry was his own affair and a thing apart,

40

THE DWELLER IN THE INNERMOST.

like the fact that he collected coins or earned his living as a hatter. But Tennyson really belonged to an older tradition, the tradition that believed that the poet, the appointed "Vates," was a recognized and public figure like the bard or jester at the mediæval courts, like the prophet in the old Commonwealth of Israel. In Tennyson's work appeared for the last time in English history this notion of the stately and public and acknowledged poet : it was the lay of the last minstrel.

Now there is in Watts, gentle and invisible as he is, something that profoundly responds to that spirit. Leighton, like Browning, was a courtier and man of the world : Millais, like Browning, was a good fellow and an ordinary gentleman : but Watts has more of Tennyson in him ; he believes in a great priesthood of art. He believes in a certain pure and childish publicity. If anyone suggested that before a man ventured to paint pictures or to daub with plaster he should be initiated with some awful rites in some vast and crowded national temple, should swear to work worthily before some tremendous altar or over some symbolic flame, Millais would have laughed heartily at the idea and Leighton also. But it would not seem either absurd or unreasonable to Watts. In the thick of this smoky century he is living in a clear age of heroes.

Watts' relations to Tennyson were indeed very characteristic of what was finest, and at the same time quaintest, in the two men. The painter, with a typical sincerity, took the poet seriously, I had almost said literally, in his daily life, and liked him to live up to his poetry. The poet, with that queer sulky humour which gave him, perhaps, more breadth than Watts, but less strength, said, after reading some acid and unjust criticisms, " I wish I had never written a line." "Come," said Watts, "you wouldn't like 'King Arthur' to talk like that." Tennyson paused a moment and then spread out his fingers. "Well," he said, "what do you expect? It's all the gout." The artist, with a characteristic power of juvenile and immortal hero-worship, tells this story as an instance of the fundamental essence of odd magnanimity and sombre geniality in Tennyson. It is such an instance and a very good one: but it is also an instance of the sharp logical idealism, of the prompt poetic candour of Watts. He asked Tennyson to be King Arthur, and it never occurred to him to think that he was asking Addison to be Cato, or Massinger to be Saint Dorothy. The incident is a fine tribute to a friendship.

The real difficulty which many cultivated people have in the matter of Watts' allegorical pictures is far more difficult. It is indeed nothing else but the great general reaction against allegorical art which has arisen during the last artistic period. The only way in which we can study, with any real sincerity, the allegoric art of Watts is to ask to what is really due the objection to allegory which has thus arisen. The real objection to allegory is, it may roughly be said, founded upon the conception that allegory involves one art imitating another. This is, up to a certain point, true. To paint a figure in a blue robe and call her Necessity, and then paint a small figure in a yellow robe and call it Invention; to put the second on the knee of the first, and then say that you are enunciating the sublime and eternal truth, that Necessity is the mother of Invention, this is indeed an idle and foolish affair. It is saying in six weeks' work with brush and palette knife what could be said much better in six words. And there can be no reasonable dispute that of this character were a considerable

GEORGE   MEREDITH.

number of the allegorical pictures that have crowded
the galleries and sprawled over the ceilings of ancient
and modern times. Of such were the monstrous
pictures of Rubens, which depicted a fat Religion and
a bloated Temperance dancing before some foreign
conqueror; of such were the florid designs of the
eighteenth century, which showed Venus and Apollo
encouraging Lord Peterborough to get over the
inconvenience of his breastplate; of such, again, were
the meek Victorian allegories which showed Mercy
and Foresight urging men to found a Society for the
Preservation of Young Game. Of such were almost
all the allegories which have dominated the art of
Europe for many centuries back. Of such, most
emphatically, the allegories of Watts are not. They
are not mere pictorial forms, combined as in a kind
of cryptogram to express theoretic views or relations.
They are not proverbs or verbal relations rendered
with a cumbrous exactitude in oil and Chinese white.
They are not, in short, the very thing that the oppo-
nents of Watts and his school say that they are. They
are not merely literary. There is one definite current
conception on which this idea that Watts' allegorical
art is merely literary is eventually based. It is based
upon the idea that lies at the root of rationalism, at
the root of useless logomachies, at the root, in no small
degree, of the whole modern evil. It is based on the
assumption of the perfection of language. Every
religion and every philosophy must, of course, be based
on the assumption of the authority or the accuracy
of something. But it may well be questioned whether
it is not saner and more satisfactory to ground our
faith on the infallibility of the Pope, or the infallibility of the Book of Mormon, than on this astounding
modern dogma of the infallibility of human speech.
Every time one man says to another, " Tell us plainly

what you mean ? " he is assuming the infallibility
of language : that is to say, he is assuming that
there is a perfect scheme of verbal expression for all
the internal moods and meanings of men. Whenever
a man says to another, "Prove your case ; defend
your faith," he is assuming the infallibility of language : that is to say, he is assuming that a man has a
word for every reality in earth, or heaven, or hell.
He knows that there are in the soul tints more
bewildering, more numberless, and more nameless
than the colours of an autumn forest ; he knows that
there are abroad in the world and doing strange and
terrible service in it crimes that have never been
condemned and virtues that have never been christened.
Yet he seriously believes that these things can every
one of them, in all their tones and semi-tones, in all
their blends and unions, be accurately represented
by an arbitrary system of grunts and squeals. He
believes that an ordinary civilized stockbroker can really
produce out of his own inside noises which denote all
the mysteries of memory and all the agonies of desire.
Whenever, on the other hand, a man rebels faintly or
vaguely against this way of speaking, whenever a
man says that he cannot explain what he means, and
that he hates argument, that his enemy is misrepre-
senting him, but he cannot explain how ; that man is
a true sage, and has seen into the heart of the real
nature of language. Whenever a man refuses to be
caught by some dilemma about reason and passion,
or about reason and faith, or about fate and free-will,
he has seen the truth. Whenever a man declines to be
cornered as an egotist, or an altruist, or any such
modern monster, he has seen the truth. For the truth
is that language is not a scientific thing at all, but
wholly an artistic thing, a thing invented by hunters,
and killers, and such artists long before science was

44

ORPHEUS AND EURYDICE.

dreamed of. The truth is simply that—that the
tongue is not a reliable instrument, like a theodolite
or a camera. The tongue is most truly an unruly
member, as the wise saint has called it, a thing poetic
and dangerous, like music or fire.

Now we can easily imagine an alternative state of
things, roughly similar to that produced in Watts'
allegories, a system, that is to say, whereby the moods
or facts of the human spirit were conveyed by something other than speech, by shapes or colours or some
such things. As a matter of fact, of course, there are
a great many other languages besides the verbal.
Descriptions of spiritual states and mental purposes
are conveyed by a variety of things, by hats, by bells,
by guns, by fires on a headland, or by jerks of the head.
In fact there does exist an example which is singularly analogous to decorative and symbolic painting.
This is a scheme of æsthetic signs or emblems, simple
indeed and consisting only of a few elemental colours,
which is actually employed to convey great lessons in
human safety and great necessities of the commonwealth. It need hardly be said that I allude to the
railway signals. They are as much a language, and
surely as solemn a language, as the colour sequence of
ecclesiastical vestments, which sets us red for martyrdom, and white for resurrection. For the green and
red of the night-signals depict the two most fundamental things of all, which lie at the back of all language. Yes and no, good and bad, safe and unsafe,
life and death. It is perfectly conceivable that a
degree of flexibility or subtlety might be introduced
into these colours so as to suggest other and more
complex meanings. We might (under the influence
of some large poetic station-masters) reach a state
of things in which a certain rich tinge of purple in
the crimson light would mean " Travel for a few

seconds at a slightly more lingering pace, that a romantic old lady in a first-class carriage may admire the scenery of the forest." A tendency towards peacock blue in the green might mean "An old gentleman with a black necktie has just drunk a glass of sherry at the station restaurant." But however much we modified or varied this colour sequence or colour language, there would remain one thing which it would be quite ridiculous and untrue to say about it. It would be quite ridiculous and untrue to say that this colour sequence was simply a symbol representing language. It would be another language : it would convey its meaning to aliens who had another word for forest, and another word for sherry, and another word for old lady. It would not be a symbol of language, a symbol of a symbol; it would be one symbol of the reality, and language would be another. That is precisely the true position touching allegorical art in general, and, above all, the allegorical art of Watts.

So long as we conceive that it is, fundamentally, the symbolizing of literature in paint, we shall certainly misunderstand it and the rare and peculiar merits, both technical and philosophical, which really characterize it. If the ordinary spectator at the art galleries finds himself, let us say, opposite a picture of a dancing flower-crowned figure in a rose-coloured robe, he feels a definite curiosity to know the title, looks it up in the catalogue, and finds that it is called, let us say, "Hope." He is immediately satisfied, as he would have been if the title had run "Portrait of Lady Warwick," a "View of Kilchurn Castle." It represents a certain definite thing, the word "hope." But what does the word "hope" represent ? It represents only a broken instantaneous glimpse of something that is immeasurably older and wilder

HOPE.

than language, that is immeasurably older and wilder than man ; a mystery to saints and a reality to wolves. To suppose that such a thing is dealt with by the word "hope," any more than America is represented by a distant view of Cape Horn, would indeed be ridiculous. It is not merely true that the word itself is, like any other word, arbitrary ; that it might as well be " pig " or " parasol " ; but it is true that the philosophical meaning of the word, in the conscious mind of man, is merely a part of something immensely larger in the unconscious mind, that the gusty light of language only falls for a moment on a fragment, and that obviously a semi-detached, unfinished fragment of a certain definite pattern on the dark tapestries of reality. It is vain and worse than vain to declaim against the allegoric, for the very word " hope " is an allegory, and the very word "allegory" is an allegory.

Now let us suppose that instead of coming before that hypothetical picture of *Hope* in conventional flowers and conventional pink robes, the spectator came before another picture. Suppose that he found himself in the presence of a dim canvas with a bowed and stricken and secretive figure cowering over a broken lyre in the twilight. What would he think ? His first thought, of course, would be that the picture was called *Despair* ; his second (when he discovered his error in the catalogue), that it has been entered under the wrong number ; his third, that the painter was mad. But if we imagine that he overcame these preliminary feelings and that as he stared at that queer twilight picture a dim and powerful sense of meaning began to grow upon him—what would he see ? He would see something for which there is neither speech nor language, which has been too vast for any eye to see and too secret for any religion to utter, even as an esoteric doctrine. Standing before that picture, he finds himself in the presence of a great truth. He perceives that there is something in man which is always apparently on the eve of disappearing, but never disappears, an assurance which is always apparently saying farewell and yet illimitably lingers, a string which is always stretched to snapping and yet never snaps. He perceives that the queerest and most delicate thing in us, the most fragile, the most fantastic, is in truth the backbone and indestructible. He knows a great moral fact : that there never was an age of assurance, that there never was an age of faith. Faith is always at a disadvantage ; it is a perpetually defeated thing which survives all its conquerors. The desperate modern talk about dark days and reeling altars, and the end of Gods and angels, is the oldest talk in the world : lamentations over the growth of agnosticism can be found in the monkish sermons of the dark ages ; horror at youthful impiety can be found in the Iliad. This is the thing that never deserts men and yet always, with daring diplomacy, threatens to desert them. It has indeed dwelt among and controlled all the kings and crowds, but only with the air of a pilgrim passing by. It has indeed warmed and lit men from the beginning of Eden with an unending glow, but it was the glow of an eternal sunset.

Here, in this dim picture, its trick is almost betrayed. No one can name this picture properly, but Watts, who painted it, has named it *Hope*. But the point is that this title is not (as those think who call it " literary ") the reality behind the symbol, but another symbol for the same thing, or, to speak yet more strictly, another symbol describing another part or aspect of the same complex reality. Two men felt a swift, violent, invisible thing in the world : one said the word " hope," the other painted a

JONAH.

picture in blue and green paint. The picture is inadequate; the word "hope" is inadequate; but between them, like two angles in the calculation of a distance, they almost locate a mystery, a mystery that for hundreds of ages has been hunted by men and evaded them. And the title is therefore not so much the substance of one of Watts' pictures, it is rather an epigram upon it. It is merely an approximate attempt to convey, by snatching up the tool of another craftsman, the direction attempted in the painter's own craft. He calls it *Hope*, and that is perhaps the best title. It reminds us among other things of a fact which is too little remembered, that faith, hope, and charity, the three mystical virtues of Christianity, are also the gayest of the virtues. Paganism, as I have suggested, is not gay, but rather nobly sad; the spirit of Watts, which is as a rule nobly sad also, here comes nearer perhaps than anywhere else to mysticism in the strict sense, the mysticism which is full of secret passion and belief, like that of Fra Angelico or Blake. But though Watts calls his tremendous reality *Hope*, we may call it many other things. Call it faith, call it vitality, call it the will to live, call it the religion of to-morrow morning, call it the immortality of man, call it self-love and vanity; it is the thing that explains why man survives all things and why there is no such thing as a pessimist. It cannot be found in any dictionary or rewarded in any commonwealth: there is only one way in which it can even be noticed and recognized. If there be anywhere a man who has really lost it, his face out of a whole crowd of men will strike us like a blow. He may hang himself or become Prime Minister; it matters nothing. The man is dead.

Now, of course the ordinary objection to allegory,

D

and it is a very sound objection, can be sufficiently
well stated by saying that the pictorial figures are mere
arbitrary symbols of the words. An allegorist of the
pompous school might paint some group of Peace
and Commerce doing something to Britannia. There
might be a figure of Commerce in a Greek robe with
a cornucopia or bag of gold or an argosy or any other
conventional symbol. But it is surely quite evident
that such a figure is a mere sign like the word commerce : the word might just as well be " dandelion,"
and the Greek lady with the cornucopia might just
as well be a Hebrew prophet standing on his head.
It is scarcely even a language : it is a cipher-code.
Nobody can maintain that the figure, taken as a figure,
makes one think of commerce, of the forces that
effect commerce, of a thousand ports, of a thousand
streets, of a thousand warehouses and bills of lading,
of a thousand excited men in black coats who certainly
would not know what to do with a cornucopia. If
we find ourselves gazing at some monument of the
fragile and eternal faith of man, at some ruined chapel,
at some nameless altar, at some scrap of old Jacobin
eloquence, we might actually find our own minds
moving in certain curves that centre in the curved
back of Watts' *Hope:* we might almost think for
ourselves of a bowed figure in the twilight, holding
to her breast something damaged but undestroyed.
But can anyone say that by merely looking at the
Stock Exchange on a busy day we should think of a
Greek lady with an argosy ? Can anyone say that
Threadneedle Street, in itself, would inspire our minds
to move in the curves which centre in a cornucopia ?
Can anyone say that a very stolid figure in a very
outlandish drapery is anything but a purely arbitrary
sign, like x or y, for such a thing as modern commerce,
for the savagery of the rich, for the hunger of the

satisfied, for the vast tachycardia or galloping of the heart that has fallen on all the great new centres of civilization, for the sudden madness of all the mills of the world ?

Watts' *Hope* does tell us something more about the nature of hope than we can be told by merely noticing that hope is shown in individual cases : that a man rehearses successful love speeches when he is in love, and takes a return ticket when he goes out to fight a duel. But the figure of Commerce with the cornucopia gives us less insight into what is behind commerce than we might get from reading a circular or staring out into the street. In the case of Commerce the figure is merely a symbol of commerce, which is a symbol. In the case of Hope the matter is quite the other way ; the figure brings us nearer to something which is not a symbol, but the reality behind symbols. In the one case we go further down towards the river's delta ; in the other, further up towards its fountain ; that at least may be called a difference. And now, suppose that our imaginary sight-seer who had seen so much of the pompous allegory of Commerce in her Grecian draperies were to see, for the second time, a second picture. Suppose he saw before him a throned figure clad in splendid, heavy scarlet and gold, above the lustre and dignity of which rose, in abrupt contrast, a face like the face of a blind beast. Suppose that as this imperial thing, with closed eyes and fat, sightless face, sat upon his magnificent seat, he let his heavy hand and feet fall, as if by a mere pulverizing accident, on the naked and god-like figures of the young, on men and women. Suppose that in the background there rose straight into the air a raw and turgid smoke, as if from some invisible and horrible sacrifice, and that by one final, fantastic, and triumphal touch this all-destroying god and king were adorned with the ears of an ass, declaring that he was royal, imperial, irresistible, and, when all is said, imbecile. Suppose that a man sick of argosies and cornucopias came before that picture, would he not say, perhaps even before he looked in the catalogue and found that the painter had called it *Mammon*, would he not say, " This is something which in spirit and in essence I have seen before, something which in spirit and in essence I have seen everywhere. That bloated, unconscious face, so heavy, so violent, so wicked, so innocent, have I not seen it at street corners, in billiard-rooms, in saloon bars, laying down the law about Chartered shares or gaping at jokes about women ? Those huge and smashing limbs, so weighty, so silly, so powerless, and yet so powerful, have I not seen them in the pompous movements, the morbid health of the prosperous in the great cities ? The hard, straight pillars of that throne, have I not seen them in the hard, straight, hideous tiers of modern warehouses and factories ? That tawny and sulky smoke, have I not seen it going up to heaven from all the cities of the coming world ? This is no trifling with argosies and Greek drapery. This is commerce. This is the home of the god himself. This is why men hate him, and why men fear him, and why men endure him."

Now, of course, it is at once obvious that this view would be very unjust to commerce ; but that modification, as a matter of fact, very strongly supports the general theory at the moment under consideration. Commerce is really an arbitrary phrase, a thing including a million motives, from the motive which makes a man drink to the motive which makes him reform ; from the motive that makes a starving man eat a horse to the motive which makes an idle man chase a butterfly. But whatever other spirits there are in commerce, there is, beyond all reasonable

MAMMON

question, in it this powerful and enduring spirit
which Watts has painted. There is, as a ruling element
in modern life, in all life, this blind and asinine
appetite for mere power. There is a spirit abroad
among the nations of the earth which drives men
incessantly on to destroy what they cannot understand, and to capture what they cannot enjoy. This,
and not commerce, is what Watts has painted. He has
painted, not the allegory of a great institution, but the
vision of a great appetite, the vision of a great motive.
It is not true that this is a picture of Commerce ;
but that Commerce and Watts' picture spring from
the same source. There does exist a certain dark and
driving force in the world ; one of its products is
this picture, another is Commerce. The picture is
not Commerce, it is Mammon. And, indeed, so
powerfully and perfectly has Watts, in this case,
realized the awful being whom he was endeavouring
to call up by his artistic incantation, that we may
even say the common positions of allegory and reality
are reversed. The fact is not that here we have an
effective presentation under a certain symbol of red
robes and smoke and a throne, of what the financial
world is, but rather that here we have something
of the truth that is hidden behind the symbol of
white waistcoats and hats on the back of the head, of
financial papers and sporting prophets, of butter
closing quiet and Pendragon being meant to win.
This is not a symbol of commerce : commerce is a
symbol of this.

In sketching this general and necessary attitude
towards the art of Watts, particularly in the matter
of allegory, I have taken deliberately these two very
famous and obvious pictures, and I have occupied,
equally deliberately, a considerable amount of space
in expounding them. It is far better in a subject so

subtle and so bewildering as the relation between art and philosophy, that we should see how our conceptions and hypotheses really get on when applied systematically and at some length to some perfectly familiar and existent object. A philosopher cannot talk about any single thing, down to a pumpkin, without showing whether he is wise or foolish; but he can easily talk about everything with anyone having any views about him beyond gloomy suspicions. But at this point I become fully conscious of another and most important kind of criticism, which has been and can be levelled against the allegories of Watts; and which must be, by the nature of things, evoked by the particular line of discussion or reflection that I have here adopted.

It may be admitted that Watts' art is not merely literary in the sense in which I have originally used the term. It may be admitted that there is truth in the general position I have sketched out—that Watts is not a man copying literature or philosophy, but rather a man copying the great spiritual and central realities which literature and philosophy also set out to copy. It may be admitted that *Mammon* is obviously an attempt to portray, not a twopenny phrase, but a great idea. But along with all these admissions it will certainly be said, by the most powerful and recent school in art criticism, that all this amounts to little more than a difference between a mean and a magnificent blunder. Pictorial art, it will be said, has no more business, as such, to portray great ideas than small ideas. Its affair is with its own technique, with the love of a great billowing line for its own sake, of a subtle and perfect tint for its own sake. If a man mistakes his trade and attends to the technique of another, the sublimity of his mind is only a very slight consolation. If I summon a paperhanger

54

DEATH CROWNING INNOCENCE.

to cover the walls, and he insists on playing the piano, it matters little whether he plays Beethoven or "The Yachmak." If I charter a pianist, and he is found drinking in the wine cellar, it matters little whether he has made his largest hole in good Burgundy or bad Marsala. If the whole of this question of great ideas and small ideas, of large atmospheres and superficial definitions, of the higher and the lower allegory—if all this be really irrelevant to the discussion of the position of a painter, then, indeed, we have been upon an idle track. As I think I shall show in a moment, this is a very inadequate view of the matter. But it does draw our attention to an aspect of the matter which must, without further delay, be discussed. That aspect, as I need hardly say, is the technique of Watts.

There is of course a certain tendency among all interesting and novel critical philosophers to talk as if they had discovered things which it is perfectly impossible that any human being could ever have denied ; to shout that the birds fly, and declare that in spite of persecution they will still assert that cows have four legs. In this way some raw pseudo-scientists talk about heredity or the physical basis of life as if it were not a thing embedded in every creed and legend, and even the very languages of men. In this way some of the new oligarchists of to-day imagine they are attacking the doctrine of human equality by pointing out that some men are stronger or cleverer than others ; as if they really believed that Danton and Washington thought that every man was the same height and had the same brains. And something of this preliminary cloud of folly or misunderstanding attaches doubtless to the question of the technical view—that is, the solely technical view—of painting. If the principle of " art for art's

sake " means simply that there is a solely technical
view of painting, and that it must be supreme on its
own ground, it appears a piece of pure madness to
suppose it other than true. Surely there never was
really a man who held that a picture that was vile in
colour and weak in drawing was a good picture because
it was a picture of Florence Nightingale ! Surely
there never was really a man who said that when
one leg in a drawing was longer than another, yet
they were both the same length because the artist
painted it for an altar-piece ! When the new critics
with a burst of music and a rocket shower of epigrams
enunciated their new criticism, they must at any rate
have meant something more than this. Undoubtedly
they did mean something more ; they meant that a
picture was not a good vehicle for moral sentiment
at all ; they meant that not only was it not the better
for having a philosophic meaning, but that it was
worse. This, if it be true, is beyond all question a
real indictment of Watts.

About the whole of this Watts controversy about
didactic art there is at least one perfectly plain and
preliminary thing to be said. It is said that art
cannot teach a lesson. This is true, and the only
proper addition is the statement that neither, for the
matter of that, can morality teach a lesson. For a
thing to be didactic, in the strict and narrow and
scholastic sense, it must be something about facts or
the physical sciences : you can only teach a lesson
about such a thing as Euclid or the making of paper
boats. The thing is quite inapplicable to the great
needs of man, whether moral or æsthetic. Nobody
ever held a class in philanthropy with fifteen million-
aires in a row writing cheques. Nobody ever held
evening continuation classes in martyrdom, or drilled
boys in a playground to die for their country. A

A STORY FROM BOCCACCIO.

picture cannot give a plain lesson in morals; neither
can a sermon. A didactic poem was a thing known
indeed among the ancients and the old Latin civilization, but as a matter of fact it scarcely ever professed
to teach people how to live the higher life. It taught
people how to keep bees.

Since we find, therefore, that ethics is like art, a
mystic and intuitional affair, the only question that
remains is, have they any kinship? If they have not,
a man is not a man, but two men and probably more :
if they have, there is, to say the least of it, at any rate
a reasonable possibility that a note in moral feeling
might have affinity with a note in art, that a curve
in law, so to speak, may repeat a curve in draughtsmanship, that there may be genuine and not artificial
correspondences between a state of morals and an
effect in painting. This would, I should tentatively
suggest, appear to be a most reasonable hypothesis.
It is not so much the fact that there is no such thing
as allegorical art, but rather the fact that there is
no art that is not allegorical. But the meanings
expressed in high and delicate art are not to be classed
under cheap and external ethical formulæ, they deal
with strange vices and stranger virtues. Art is
only unmoral in so far as most morality is immoral.
Thus Mr. Whistler when he drops a spark of perfect
yellow or violet into some glooming pool of the
nocturnal Thames is, in all probability, enunciating
some sharp and wholesome moral comment. When
the young Impressionists paint dim corners of meadows
or splashes of sunlight in the wood, this does not mean
necessarily that they are unmoral ; it may only mean
that they are a very original and sincere race of stern
young moralists.

Now if we adopt this general theory of the existence of genuine correspondences between art and

moral beauty, of the existence, that is to say, of genuine allegories, it is perfectly clear wherein the test of such genuineness must consist. It must consist in the nature of the technique. If the technique, considered as technique, is calculated to evoke in us a certain kind of pleasure, and there is an analogous pleasure in the meaning considered as meaning, then there is a true wedding of the arts. But if the pleasure in the technique be of a kind quite dissimilar in its own sphere to the pleasure in the spiritual suggestion, then it is a mechanical and unlawful union, and this philosophy, at any rate, forbids the banns. If the intellectual conceptions uttered in Michel Angelo's *Day of Judgment* in the Sistine Chapel were the effect of a perfect and faultless workmanship, but the workmanship such as we should admire in a Gothic missal or a picture by Gerard Dow, we should then say that absolute excellence in both departments did not excuse their being joined. The thing would have been a mere accident, or convenience. Just as two plotters might communicate by means of a bar or two of music, so these subtle harmonies of colour and form would have been used for their detached and private ends by the dark conspirators of morality.

Now there is nothing in the world that is really so thoroughly characteristic of Watts' technique as the fact that it does almost startlingly correspond to the structure of his spiritual sense. If such pictures as *The Dweller in the Innermost* and *Mammon* and *Diana and Endymion* and *Eve Repentant* had neither title nor author, if no one had heard of Watts or heard of Eve ; if, for the matter of that, the pictures had neither human nor animal form, it would be possible to guess something of the painter's attitude from the mere colour and line. If Watts painted an arabesque, it would be moral; if he designed a Turkey

LORD LYTTON.

carpet, it would be stoical. So individual is his
handling that his very choice and scale of colours
betray him. A man with a keen sense of the spiritual
and symbolic history of colours could guess at something about Watts from the mess on his palette. He
would see giants and the sea and cold primeval dawns
and brown earth-men and red earth-women lying
in the heaps of greens and whites and reds, like forces
in chaos before the first day of creation. A certain
queer and yet very simple blue there is, for instance,
which is like Titian's and yet not like it, which is
more lustrous and yet not less opaque, and which
manages to suggest the north rather than Titian's
south, in spite of its intensity; which suggests also
the beginning of things rather than their maturity;
a hot spring of the earth rather than Titian's opulent
summer. Then there is that tremendous autoch-
thonous red, which was the colour of Adam, whose
name was Red Earth. It is, if one may say so, the
clay in which no one works, except Watts and the
Eternal Potter. There are other colours that have
this character, a character indescribable except by
saying that they come from the palette of Creation
—a green especially that reappears through portraits,
allegories, landscapes, heroic designs, but always has
the same fierce and elfish look, like a green that has
a secret. It may be seen in the signet ring of Owen
Meredith, and in the eyes of the *Dweller in the Inner
most*. But all these colours have, as I say, the first
and most characteristic and most obvious of the
mental qualities of Watts; they are simple and like
things just made by God. Nor is it, I think, altogether
fanciful to push this analogy or harmony a step
further and to see in the colours and the treatment
of them the other side or typical trait which I have
frequently mentioned as making up the identity

of the painter. He is, as I say, a stoic; therefore to some extent, at least, a pagan; he has no special sympathy with Celtic intensity, with Catholic mysticism, with Romanticism, with all the things that deal with the cells of the soul, with agonies and dreams. And I think a broad distinction between the finest pagan and the finest Christian point of view may be found in such an approximate phrase as this, that paganism deals always with a light shining on things, Christianity with a light shining through them. That is why the whole Renaissance colouring is opaque, the whole Pre-Raphaelite colouring transparent. The very sky of Rubens is more solid than the rocks of Giotto : it is like a noble cliff of immemorial blue marble. The artists of the devout age seemed to regret that they could not make the light show through everything, as it shows through the little wood in the wonderful *Nativity* of Botticelli. And that is why, again, Christianity, which has been attacked so strangely as dull and austere, invented the thing which is more intoxicating than all the wines of the world, stained-glass windows.

Now Watts, with all his marvellous spirituality, or rather because of his peculiar type of marvellous spirituality, has the Platonic, the philosophic, rather than the Catholic order of mysticism. And it can scarcely be a coincidence that here again we feel it to be something that could almost be deduced from the colours if they were splashed at random about a canvas. The colours are mystical, but they are not transparent ; that is, not transparent in the very curious but unmistakable sense in which the colours of Botticelli or Rossetti are transparent. What they are can only be described as iridescent. A curious lustre or glitter, conveyed chiefly by a singular and individual brushwork, lies over all his great pictures.

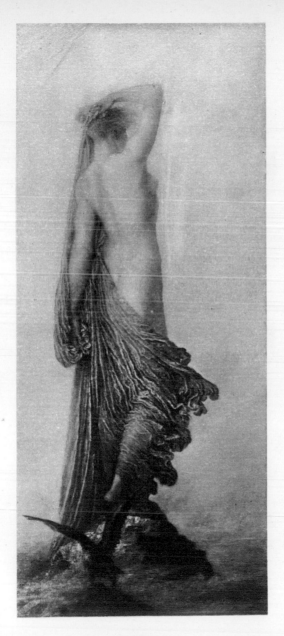

DAWN.

GEORGE FREDERICK WATTS

It is the dawn of things : it is the glow of the primal sense of wonder ; it is the sun of the childhood of the world ; it is the light that never was on sea or land ; but still it is a light shining on things, not shining through them. It is a light which exhibits and does honour to this world, not a light that breaks in upon this world to bring it terror or comfort, like the light that suddenly peers round the corner of some dark Gothic chapel with its green or golden or blood-red eyes. The Gothic artists, as I say, would have liked men's bodies to become like burning glass (as the figures in their windows do), that the light might pass through them. There is no fear of light passing through Watts' *Cain*.

These analogies must inevitably appear fantastic to those who do not accept the general hypothesis of a possible kinship between pictorial and moral harmonies in the psychology of men ; but to those who do accept this not very extravagant hypothesis, it may, I think, be repeated by way of summary, that the purely technical question of Watts' colour scheme does provide us, at least suggestively, with these two parallels. Watts, so far as his moral and mental attitude can be expressed by any phrases of such brevity, has two main peculiarities : first, a large infantile poetry which delights in things fresh, raw, and gigantic ; second, a certain Greek restraint and agnostic severity, which throws a strong light on this world as it is. The colours he uses have also two main peculiarities . first, a fresh, raw, and, as it were, gigantic character ; secondly, an opaque reflected light, unlike the mediæval lighting, a strong light thrown on this world as it is.

Similar lines of comparison, so far as they appear to possess any value, could, of course, be very easily pointed out in connexion with the character of

Watts' draughtsmanship. That his lines are simple and powerful, that both in strength and weakness they are candid and austere, that they are not Celtic, not Catholic, and not romantic lines of draughtsmanship, would, I think, appear sufficiently clear to anyone who has any instinct for this mode of judgment at all. In the matter of line and composition, of course, the same general contention applies as in the case of colour. The curve of the bent figure of *Hope*, considered simply as a curve, half repeating as it does the upper curve of the globe, suggests a feeling, a sense of fear, of simplicity, of something which lies near to the nature of the idea itself, the idea which inspires the title of the picture. The splendid rushing whirlpool of curves which constitutes, as it were, the ellipse of the two figures in *Diana and Endymion* is a positive inspiration. It is, simply as a form for a picture, a mere scheme of lines, the very soul of Greece. It is simple ; it is full and free ; it follows great laws of harmony, but it follows them swiftly and at will ; it is headlong, and yet at rest, like the solid arch of a waterfall. It is a rushing and passionate meeting of two superb human figures ; and it is almost a mathematical harmony. Technically, at least, and as a matter of outlines, it is probably the artist's masterpiece.

Before we quit this second department of the temperament of Watts, as expressed in his line, mention must be made of what is beyond all question the most interesting and most supremely personal of all the elements in the painter's designs and draughtsmanship. That is, of course, his magnificent discovery of the artistic effect of the human back. The back is the most awful and mysterious thing in the universe : it is impossible to speak about it. It is the part of man that he knows nothing of ; like an

EVE REPENTANT.

outlying province forgotten by an emperor. It is a common saying that anything may happen behind our backs : transcendentally considered the thing has an eerie truth about it. Eden may be behind our backs, or Fairyland. But this mystery of the human back has again its other side in the strange impression produced on those behind : to walk behind anyone along a lane is a thing that, properly speaking, touches the oldest nerve of awe. Watts has realized this as no one in art or letters has realized it in the whole history of the world : it has made him great. There is one possible exception to his monopoly of this magnificent craze. Two thousand years before, in the dark scriptures of a nomad people, it had been said that their prophet saw the immense Creator of all things, but only saw Him from behind. I do not know whether even Watts would dare to paint that. But it reads like one of his pictures, like the most terrific of all his pictures, which he has kept veiled.

I need not instance the admirable and innumerable cases of this fine and individual effect. *Eve Repentant* (that fine picture), in which the agony of a gigantic womanhood is conveyed as it could not be conveyed by any power of visage, in the powerful contortion of the muscular and yet beautiful back, is the first that occurs to the mind. The sad and sardonic picture painted in later years, *For He had Great Possessions*— showing the young man of the Gospel loaded with his intolerable pomp of garments and his head sunken out of sight—is of course another. Others are slighter instances, like *Good Luck to your Fishing*. He has again carried the principle, in one instance, to an extreme seldom adopted, I should fancy, either by artist or man. He has painted a very graceful portrait of his wife, in which that lady's face is entirely

omitted, the head being abruptly turned away.
But it is indeed idle to multiply these instances of
the painter's hobby (if one may use the phrase) of
the worship of the human back, when all such instances have been dwarfed and overshadowed by the
one famous and tremendous instance that everyone
knows. *Love and Death* is truly a great achievement :
if it stood alone it would have made a man great.
And it fits in with a peculiar importance with the
general view I am suggesting of the Watts technique.
For the whole picture really hangs, both technically
and morally, upon one single line, a line that could
be drawn across a blank canvas, the spine-line of the
central figure of Death with its great falling garment.
The whole composition, the whole conception, and,
I was going to say, the whole moral of the picture,
could be deduced from that single line. The moral
of the picture (if moral were the right phrase for
these things) is, it is scarcely necessary to point out,
the monument of about as noble a silence and sup-
pression as the human mind ever bent itself to in its
pride. It is the great masterpiece of agnosticism.
In that picture agnosticism—not the cheap and queru-
lous incredulity which abuses the phrase, but loyal
and consistent agnosticism, which is as willing to
believe good as evil and to harbour faith as doubt—
has here its great and pathetic place and symbol
in the house of the arts. It is the artistic embodiment
of reverent ignorance at its highest, fully as much as
the Divine Comedy is the artistic embodiment of
Christianity.

Technically, in a large number of cases, it is probably
true that Watts' portraits, or some of them at least,
are his most successful achievements. But here also
we find our general conclusion : for if his portraits
are his best pictures, it is certainly not because they

LOVE AND DEATH.

are merely portraits; if they are in some cases better
than his symbolic designs, it is certainly not because
they are less symbolic. In his gallery of great men,
indeed, we find Watts almost more himself than
anywhere else. Most men are allegorical when
they are painting allegories, but Watts is allegorical
when he is painting an old alderman. A change
passes over that excellent being, a change of a kind
to which aldermen are insufficiently inured. He
begins to resolve into the primal elements, to become
dust and the shadow, to become the red clay of
Adam and the wind of God. His eyes become, in
spite of his earnest wish, the fixed stars in the sky of
the spirit; his complexion begins to show, not
the unmeaning red of portraits and miniatures, but
that secret and living red which is within us, and
which is the river of man. The astounding manner
in which Watts has, in some cases, treated his sitters
is one of the most remarkable things about his
character. He is not (it is almost absurd to have to
mention such a thing about the almost austere old
democrat) a man likely to flatter a sitter in any
worldly or conventional sense. Nor is he, for the
matter of that, a man likely to push compliments
far from any motive : he is a strict, and I should
infer a candid, man. The type of virtues he chiefly
admires and practises are the reverse of those which
would encourage a courtier or even a universalist.
But he scarcely ever paints a man without making
him about five times as magnificent as he really
looks. The real men appear, if they present themselves afterwards, like mean and unsympathetic sketches
from the Watts original.

The fact is that this indescribable primalism,
which we have noted as coming out in the designs,
in the titles, and in Watts' very oil-colours, is present

in this matter in a most extraordinary way. Watts
does not copy men at all : he makes them over again.
He dips his hand in the clay of chaos and begins to
model a man named William Morris or a man named
Richard Burton : he is assisted, no doubt, in some
degree by a quaint old text-book called Reality,
with its stiff but suggestive woodcuts and its shrewd
and simple old hints. But the most that can be said
for the portraiture is that Watts asks a hint to come
and stop with him, puts the hint in a chair in his
studio and stares at him. The thing that comes out
at last upon the canvas is not generally a very precise
picture of the sitter, though, of course, it is almost
always a very accurate picture of the universe.

And yet while this, on the one side, is true enough,
the portraits are portraits, and very fine portraits.
But they are dominated by an element which is the
antithesis of the whole tendency of modern art, that
tendency which for want of a better word we have
to call by the absurd name of optimism. It is not,
of course, in reality a question of optimism in the
least, but of an illimitable worship and wonder
directed towards the fact of existence. There is a
great deal of difference between the optimism which
says that things are perfect and the optimism which
merely says (with a more primeval modesty) that they
are very good. One optimism says that a one-legged
man has two legs because it would be so dreadful
if he had not. The other optimism says that the fact
that the one-legged was born of a woman, has a
soul, has been in love, and has stood alive under
the stars, is a fact so enormous and thrilling that, in
comparison, it does not matter whether he has one
leg or five. One optimism says that this is the best
of all possible worlds. The other says that it is
certainly not the best of all possible worlds, but

WILLIAM MORRIS.

it is the best of all possible things that a world should be possible. Watts, as has been more than once more or less definitely suggested, is dominated throughout by this prehistoric wonder. A man to him, especially a great man, is a thing to be painted as Fra Angelico painted angels, on his knees. He has indeed, like many brilliant men in the age that produced Carlyle and Ruskin, an overwhelming tendency to hero worship. That worship had not, of course, in the case of these men any trace of that later and more denaturalized hero-worship, the tendency to worship madmen—to dream of vast crimes as one dreams of a love-affair, and to take the malformation of the soul to be the only originality. To the Carlylean (and Watts has been to some by no means inconsiderable extent a Carlylean), to the Carlylean the hero, the great man, was a man more human than humanity itself. In worshipping him you were worshipping humanity in a sacrament : and Watts seems to express in almost every line of his brush this ardent and reverent view of the great man. He overdoes it. Tennyson, fine as he was both physically and mentally, was not quite so much of a demi-god as Watts' splendid pictures would seem to suggest. Many other sitters have been sub- jected, past all recognition, to this kind of devout and ethereal caricature. But the essential of the whole matter was that the attitude of Watts was one which might almost be called worship. It was not, of course, that he always painted men as handsome in the conventional sense, or even as handsome as they were. William Morris impressed most people as a very handsome man : in Watts' marvellous portrait, so much is made of the sanguine face, the bold stare, the almost volcanic suddenness of the emergence of the head from the dark green background, that the effect of ordinary good looks, on which many of Morris's intimates would probably have prided themselves, is in some degree lost. Carlyle, again, when he saw the painter's fine rendering of him, said with characteristic surliness that he " looked like a mad labourer." Conventionally speaking, it is of course, therefore, to be admitted that the sitters did not always come off well. But the exaggeration or the distortion, if exaggeration or distortion there were, was always effected in obedience to some almost awestruck notion of the greatness or goodness of the great or good sitter. The point is not whether Watts sometimes has painted men as ugly as they were painted by the primary religious painters ; the point is, as I have said, that he painted as they did, on his knees. Now no one thinks that Mr. Sargent paints the Misses Wertheimer on his knees. His grimness and decision of drawing and colouring are not due to a sacred optimism. But those of Watts are due to this : are due to an intense conviction that there is within the sitter a great reality which has to give up its secret before he leaves the seat or the model's throne. Hence come the red violent face and minatory eyes of William Morris : the painter sought to express, and he did most successfully express, the main traits and meaning of Morris— the appearance of a certain plain masculine passion in the realm of decorative art. Morris was a man who wanted good wall-papers, not as a man wants a coin of the Emperor Constantine, which was the cloistered or abnormal way in which men had commonly devised such things : he wanted good wall-papers as a man wants beer. He clamoured for art : he brawled for it. He asserted the perfectly virile and ordinary character of the appetite for beauty. And he possessed and developed a power of moral violence on pure

68

DANTE GABRIEL ROSSETTI.

matters of taste which startled the flabby world of connoisseurship and opened a new era. He grew furious with furniture and denounced the union of wrong colours as men denounce an adultery. All this is expressed far more finely than in these clumsy sentences in that living and leonine head in the National Portrait Gallery. It is exactly the same with Carlyle. Watts' Carlyle is immeasurably more subtle and true than the Carlyle of Millais, which simply represents him as a shaggy, handsome, magnificent old man. The uglier Carlyle of Watts has more of the truth about him, the strange combination of a score of sane and healthy visions and views, with something that was not sane, which bloodshot and embittered them all, the great tragedy of the union of a strong countryside mind and body with a disease of the vitals and something like a disease of the spirit. In fact, Watts painted Carlyle " like a mad labourer " because Carlyle was a mad labourer.

This general characteristic might of course be easily traced in all the portraits one by one. If space permitted, indeed, such a process might be profitable ; for while we take careful note of all the human triviality of faces, the one thing that we all tend to forget is that divine and common thing which Watts celebrates. It is the misfortune of the non-religious ages that they tend to cultivate a sense of individuality, not only at the expense of religion, but at the expense of humanity itself. For the modern portrait-painter not only does not see the image of God in his sitters, he does not even see the image of man. His object is not to insist on the glorious and solemn heritage which is common to Sir William Harcourt and Mr. Albert Chevalier, to Count Tolstoy and Mr. Wanklyn, that is the glorious and solemn heritage of a nose and two eyes and a mouth. The effort of the dashing modern is rather to make each of these features individual almost to the point of being incredible : it is his desire to paint the mouth whose grimace is inimitable, the eyes that could be only in one head, and the nose that never was on sea or land. There is value in this purely personal treatment, but something in it so constantly lost : the quality of the common humanity. The new art gallery is too like a museum of freaks, it is too wild and wonderful, like a realistic novel. Watts errs undoubtedly on the other side. He makes all his portraits too classical. It may seem like a paradox to say that he makes them too human; but humanity is a *classis* and therefore classical. He recurs too much to the correct type which includes all men. He has, for instance, a worship of great men so complete that it makes him tend in the direction of painting them all alike. There may be too much of Browning in his Tennyson, too much of Tennyson in his Browning. There is certainly a touch of Manning in his John Stuart Mill, and a touch of the Minotaur in many of his portraits of Imperial politicians. While he celebrates the individual with a peculiar insight, it is nevertheless always referred to a general human type. We feel when we look at even the most extraordinary of Watts' portraits, as, for instance, the portrait of Lord Stratford de Redcliffe, that before Lord Stratford de Redcliffe was born, and apart from that fact, there was such a thing as a human being. When we look at a brilliant modern canvas like that of Mr. Sargent's portrait of Wertheimer, we do not feel that any human being analogous to him had of necessity existed. We feel that Mr. Wertheimer might have been created before the stars. Watts has a tendency to resume his characters into his background as if they were half returning

70

THOMAS CARLYLE.

to the forces of nature. In his more successful portraits the actual physical characteristics of the sitter
appear to be something of the nature of artistic
creations ; they are decorative and belong to a whole.
We feel that he has filled in the fiery orange of Swinburne's hair as one might fill in a gold or copper
panel. We know that he was historically correct in
making the hair orange, but we cannot get rid of a
haunting feeling that if his scheme had been a little
different he would have made it green. This indescribable sentiment is particularly strong in the case
of the portrait of Rossetti. Rossetti is dressed in a
dark green coat which perfectly expresses his sumptuous
Pre-Raphaelite affectation. But we do not feel that
Rossetti has adopted the dark green coat to suit his
dark red beard. We rather feel that if anyone had
seized Rossetti and forcibly buttoned him up in the
dark green coat he would have grown the red beard
by sheer force of will.

Before we quit the subject of portraiture a word
ought to be said about two exceedingly noble portraits,
those of Matthew Arnold and Cardinal Manning.
The former is interesting because, as an able critic
said somewhere (I wish I could remember who he was
or where he wrote), this is the one instance of Watts
approaching tentatively a man whom he in all reasonable probability did not understand. In this particular case the picture is a hundred times better for
that. The portrait-painter of Matthew Arnold obviously ought not to understand him, since he did
not understand himself. And the bewilderment
which the artist felt for those few hours reproduced
in a perfect, almost in an immortal, picture the
bewilderment which the sitter felt from the cradle to
the grave. The bewilderment of Matthew Arnold
was more noble and faithful than most men's certainty,

and Watts has not failed to give that nobility a place even greater perhaps than that which he would have given to it had he been working on that fixed theory of admiration in which he dealt with Tennyson or Morris. The sad sea-blue eyes of Matthew Arnold seemed to get near to the fundamental sadness of blue. It is a certain eternal bleakness in the colour which may for all I know have given rise to the legend of blue devils. There are times at any rate when the bluest heavens appear only blue with those devils. The portrait of Cardinal Manning is worth a further and special notice, because it is an illustration of the fact to which I have before alluded : the fact that while Watts in one sense always gets the best out of his sitters, he does not by any means always get the handsomest out of them. Manning was a singularly fine-looking man, even in his emaciation. A friend of mine, who was particularly artistic both by instinct and habits, gazed for a long time at a photograph of the terrible old man clad in those Cardinal's robes and regalia in which he exercised more than a Cardinal's power, and said reflectively, " He would have made his fortune as a model." A great many of the photographs of Manning, indeed almost any casual glimpses of him, present him as more beautiful than he appears in Watts' portrait. To the ordinary onlooker there was behind the wreck of flesh and the splendid skeleton the remains of a very handsome English gentleman ; relics of one who might have hunted foxes and married an American heiress. Watts has no eyes for anything except that sublime vow which he would himself repudiate, that awful Church which he would himself disown. He exaggerates the devotionalism of Manning. He is more ascetic than the ascetics ; more Catholic than Catholicism. Just so, he would be, if he were painting the Sheik-el-Islam, more Moslem than the Mohammedans. He has no eyes but for ideas.

Watts' allegories and Watts' portraits exhaust the subject of his art. It is true that he has on rare occasions attempted pictures merely reproducing the externals of the ordinary earth. It is characteristic of him that he should have once, for no apparent reason in particular, painted a picture of two cart-horses and a man. It is still more characteristic of him that this one picture of a trivial group in the street should be so huge as to dwarf many of his largest and most transcendental canvases; that the incidental harmless drayman should be more gigantic than the Prince of this World or Adam or the Angel of Death. He condescends to a detail and makes the detail more vast than a cosmic allegory. One picture, called "The First Oyster," he is reported to have painted in response to a challenge which accused him or his art of lacking altogether the element of humour. The charge is interesting, because it suggests a comparison with the similar charge commonly brought against Gladstone. In both charges there is an element of truth, though not complete truth. Watts proved no doubt that he was not wholly without humour by this admirable picture. Gladstone proved that he was not wholly without humour by his reply to Mr. Chaplin, by his singing of "Doo-dah," and by his support of a grant to the Duke of Coburg. But both men were singularly little possessed by the mood or the idea of humour. To them had been in peculiar fullness revealed the one great truth which our modern thought does not know and which it may possibly perish through not knowing. They knew that to enjoy life means to take it seriously. There is an eternal kinship between solemnity and high spirits, and almost the very name of it is Gladstone. Its other name is Watts. They knew that not only life, but every detail of life, is most a pleasure when it is studied with the gloomiest intensity. They knew that the men who collect beetles are jollier than the men who kill them, and that the men who worshipped beetles (in ancient Egypt) were probably the jolliest of all. The startling cheerfulness of the old age of Gladstone, the startling cheerfulness of the old age of Watts, are both entirely redolent of this exuberant seriousness, this uproarious gravity. They were as happy as the birds, because, like the birds, they were untainted by the disease of laughter. They are as awful and philosophical as children at play : indeed they remind us of a truth true for all of us, though capable of misunderstanding, that the great aim of a man's life is to get into his second childhood.

Of his work we have concluded our general survey. It has been hard in conducting such a survey to avoid the air of straying from the subject. But the greatest hardness of the subject is that we cannot stray from the subject. This man has attempted, whether he has succeeded or no, to paint such pictures of such things that no one shall be able to get outside them ; that everyone should be lost in them for ever like wanderers in a mighty park. Whether we strike a match or win the Victoria Cross, we are still giants sprawling in Chaos. Whether we hide in a monastery or thunder on a platform, we are still standing in the Court of Death. If any experience at all is genuine, it affects the philosophy of these pictures ; if any halfpenny stamp supports them, they are the better pictures ; if any dead cat in a dust-bin contradicts them, they are the worse pictures. This is the great pathos and the great dignity of philosophy and theology. Men talk of philosophy and theology as if they were something specialistic and arid and

GOOD LUCK TO YOUR FISHING.

academic. But philosophy and theology are not only the only democratic things, they are democratic to the point of being vulgar, to the point, I was going to say, of being rowdy. They alone admit all matters ; they alone lie open to all attacks. All other sciences may, while studying their own, laugh at the rag-tag and bobtail of other sciences. An astronomer may sneer at animalculæ, which are very like stars ; an entomologist may scorn the stars, which are very like animalculæ. Physiologists may think it dirty to grub about in the grass ; botanists may think it dirtier to grub about in an animal's inside. But there is nothing that is not relevant to these more ancient studies. There is no detail, from buttons to kangaroos, that does not enter into the gay confusion of philosophy. There is no fact of life, from the death of a donkey to the General Post Office, which has not its place to dance and sing in, in the glorious Carnival of theology.

Therefore I make no apology if I have asked the reader, in the course of these remarks, to think about things in general. It is not I, but George Frederick Watts, who asks the reader to think about things in general. If he has not done this, he has failed. If he has not started in us such trains of reflection as I am now concluding and many more and many better, he has failed. And this brings me to my last word. Now and again Watts has failed. I am afraid that it may possibly be inferred from the magniloquent language which I have frequently, and with a full consciousness of my act, applied to this great man, that I think the whole of his work technically triumphant. Clearly it is not. For I believe that often he has scarcely known what he was doing ; I believe that he has been in the dark when the lines came wrong ; that he has been still deeper in the dark and things came right. As I have already pointed out, the vague lines which his mere physical instinct would make him draw, have in them the curves of the Cosmos. His automatic manual action was, I think, certainly a revelation to others, certainly a revelation to himself. Standing before a dark canvas upon some quiet evening, he has made lines and something has happened. In such an hour the strange and splendid phrase of the Psalm he has literally fulfilled. He has gone on because of the word of meekness and truth and of righteousness. And his right hand has taught him terrible things.